South Huntington Pub. Lib.
145 Pidgeon Hill Rd.
Huntington Sta., N.Y. 11746

MAJOR AMERICAN IMMIGRATION

MASON CREST PUBLISHERS • PHILADELPHIA

Four Native American horsemen watch settlers arrive in the American West in this painting by Frederic Remington.

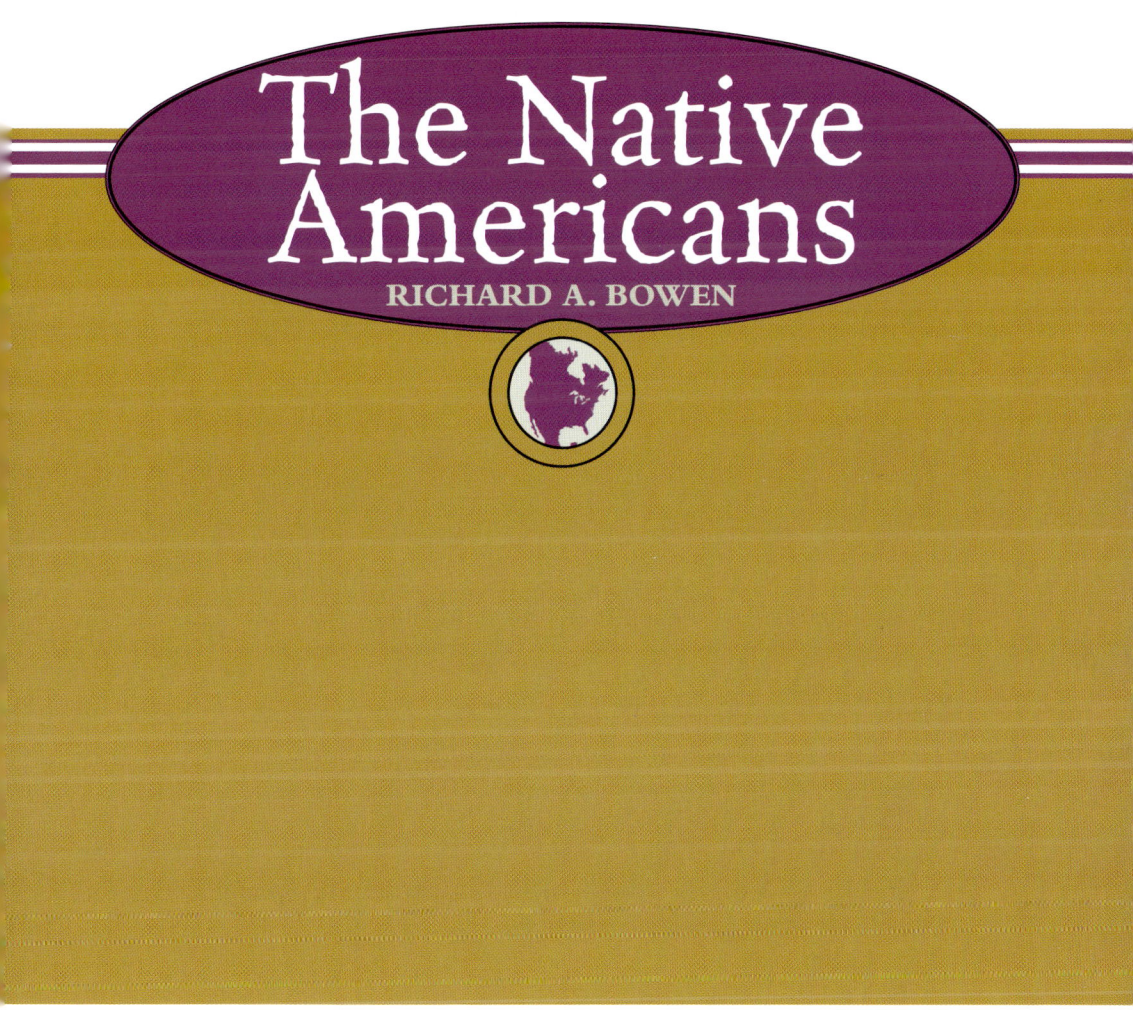

MAJOR AMERICAN IMMIGRATION

MASON CREST PUBLISHERS • PHILADELPHIA

Mason Crest Publishers
370 Reed Road
Broomall PA 19008
www.masoncrest.com

Copyright © 2009 by Mason Crest Publishers. All rights reserved.
Printed and bound in Malaysia.

First printing

1 3 5 7 9 8 6 4 2

Library of Congress Cataloging-in-Publication Data

  Bowen, Richard A.
    The Native Americans / Richard A. Bowen.
      p. cm. — (Major American immigration)
    Includes index.
    ISBN 978-1-4222-0615-7 (hardcover)
    ISBN 978-1-4222-0682-9 (pbk.)
  1. Indians of North America—Juvenile literature. 2. Paleo-Indians—Juvenile literature. I. Title.
    E77.4.M66 2008
    970.004'97—dc22
                                 2008026016

Table of Contents

Introduction: America's Ethnic Heritage
    Barry Moreno 7
1 The Story of Black Elk 11
2 Before European Dominance 21
3 European Contact 29
4 The Natives of the West 37
5 The Plateau Indians 45
6 The Subarctic People 51

Famous Native Americans 56

Chronology 57

Glossary 58

Further Reading 60

Internet Resources 61

Index 62

MAJOR AMERICAN IMMIGRATION

THE AFRICAN AMERICANS

THE ARAB-AMERICANS

THE CHINESE AMERICANS

CITIZENSHIP: RIGHTS AND RESPONSIBILITIES

THE CUBAN AMERICANS

THE GERMAN AMERICANS

HISTORY OF AMERICAN IMMIGRATION

THE IRISH-AMERICANS

THE ITALIAN AMERICANS

THE JAPANESE AMERICANS

THE JEWISH AMERICANS

THE KOREAN AMERICANS

THE MEXICAN AMERICANS

THE NATIVE AMERICANS

THE POLISH AMERICANS

THE RUSSIAN AMERICANS

INTRODUCTION

America's Ethnic Heritage

**Barry Moreno, librarian
Statue of Liberty/
Ellis Island National Monument**

Ethnic diversity is one of the most striking characteristics of the American identity. In the United States the Bureau of the Census officially recognizes 122 different ethnic groups. North America's population had grown by leaps and bounds, starting with the American Indian tribes and nations—the continent's original people—and increasing with the arrival of the European colonial migrants who came to these shores during the 16th and 17th centuries. Since then, millions of immigrants have come to America from every corner of the world.

But the passage of generations and the great distance of America from the "Old World"—Europe, Africa, and Asia—has in some cases separated immigrant peoples from their roots. The struggle to succeed in America made it easy to forget past traditions. Further, the American spirit of freedom, individualism, and equality gave Americans a perspective quite different from the view of life shared by residents of the Old World.

Immigrants of the 19th and 20th centuries recognized this at once. Many tried to "Americanize" themselves by tossing away their peasant clothes and dressing American-style even before reaching their new homes in the cities or the countryside of America. It was not so easy to become part of America's culture, however. For many immigrants, learning English was quite a hurdle. In fact, most older immigrants clung to the old ways, preferring to speak their native languages and follow their familiar customs and traditions. This was easy to do when ethnic neighborhoods abounded in large North American cities like New York, Montreal, Philadelphia, Chicago, Toronto, Boston, Cleveland, St. Louis, New Orleans and San Francisco. In rural areas, farm families—many of them Scandinavian, German, or Czech—established their own tightly knit communities. Thus foreign languages and dialects, religious beliefs, Old World customs, and certain class distinctions flourished.

The most striking changes occurred among the children of immigrants, whose hopes and dreams were different from those of their parents. They began breaking away from the Old World customs, perhaps as a reaction to the embarrassment of being labeled "foreigner." They badly wanted to be Americans, and assimilated more easily than their parents and grandparents. They learned to speak English without a foreign accent, to dress and act like other Americans. The assimilation of the children of immigrants was encouraged by social contact—games, schools, jobs, and military service—which further broke down the barriers between immigrant groups and hastened the process of Americanization. Along the way, many family traditions were lost or abandoned.

INTRODUCTION

Today, the pride that Americans have in their ethnic roots is one of the abiding strengths of both the United States and Canada. It shows that the theory which called America a "melting pot" of the world's people was never really true. The thought that a single "American" would emerge from the combination of these peoples has never happened, for Americans have grown more reluctant than ever before to forget the struggles of their ethnic forefathers. The growth of cultural studies and genealogical research indicates that Americans are anxious not to entirely lose this identity, whether it is English, French, Chinese, African, Mexican, or some other group. There is an interest in tracing back the family line as far as records or memory will take them. In a sense, this has made Americans a divided people; proud to be Americans, but proud also of their ethnic roots.

As a result, many Americans have welcomed a new identity, that of the hyphenated American. This unique description has grown in usage over the years and continues to grow as more Americans recognize the importance of family heritage. In the end, this is an appreciation of America's great cultural heritage and its richness of its variety.

Buffalo graze in the Black Hills. The life story of an Oglala Sioux named Black Elk provides a great amount of information about Native American life on the Great Plains during the 19th century.

1 The Story of Black Elk

Black Elk was born in 1863 on the Little Powder River in what is now present-day Montana. When he was five years old, he was riding along a creek on horseback carrying a bow and arrows. A thunderstorm was coming up. He saw a kingbird on a limb and thought he would shoot it, but a strange thing happened. The bird said to him, "Listen! A voice is calling you!" He looked up. Two men were coming down from the clouds, headfirst, toward him. They sang, "Behold, a sacred voice is calling you. All over the sky, a sacred voice is calling." Then, they suddenly veered away toward the west, turned into two geese, and were gone. The storm came in with a roaring wind. It was the first time Black Elk had had a *vision*.

When Black Elk was nine years old, he was riding with some boys, and they stopped to water their horses. When Black Elk jumped off his horse, his legs crumpled under him. His friends brought him back to the village, and his mother and father took him into their tepee. His legs were hurting and they became swollen. When he was lying in his bed, Black Elk looked up; he saw the two men he had seen before coming down from the clouds. This time, each carried a long spear from which lightning flashed. They said, "Hurry! Come! Your Grandfathers are calling you!" It was then that he had the greatest vision of his life. It showed him the Earth's four quarters, the "hoop"

11

of the nation, with the flowering tree of life at the center, the ancient Grandfathers, and the future destruction of the Lakota (Oglala Sioux) people. The vision lasted 12 days. Everyone thought he was dying. His parents called the medicine man, Whirlwind Chaser, who brought Black Elk back from his trance. Black Elk did not want to tell anyone about the vision because he thought no one would believe him.

The first time Black Elk saw a white person (the Sioux called whites Wasichus) was when his people were camped near Fort Robinson in Montana. It was winter, and the children were playing in the snow. Some of the boys climbed the fort's flagpole and chopped it off near the top. Soldiers from the fort came and surrounded the people with guns. Red Cloud, their chief, stood before the soldiers without a weapon and told them that the boys who damaged the flagpole would be punished. He asked the soldiers if they ever did foolish things as boys. He said it was wrong for them to shoot adults for something the children had done. Fortunately, the soldiers returned to their fort and no one was hurt.

When Black Elk was 11 years old, he found out Pahushka (Lieutenant Colonel George Armstrong Custer) was coming to their Black Hills homeland with many soldiers. They were coming to look for "the yellow metal that makes the Wasichus crazy"—gold. Black Elk said, "Our people knew there was yellow metal in chunks up there; but they did not bother with it because it was not good for anything." The soldiers held a council with the Indians to talk about digging gold. The whites wanted to "lease" the land. If the Indians did not allow them to

Red Cloud was a Sioux chief of the 19th century. Angry at the forts built by white Americans on his tribal land, Red Cloud led a successful war against the U.S. soldiers. In 1868, after two bloody years of fighting, the U.S. government asked for peace. In the Treaty of Fort Laramie, the government agreed not to allow white settlers into the Black Hills, the sacred lands of the Sioux. Unfortunately, this promise would be broken within six years.

look for gold, they said they would take the land anyway. Black Elk recalled, "It made me sad to hear this. It was such a good place to play, and the people were always happy in that country. The Wasichus had made a treaty with Red Cloud [in 1868] that said [the land] would be ours as long as the grass should grow and the water flow." After the council, more and more white settlers came to the Black Hills, where they began to establish towns.

The next winter, the soldiers told the people they had to come and live in the "Soldier's Town" (the fort) or there would be trouble. Crazy Horse, Black Elk's cousin and chief of the Oglala Sioux, was camped on the Powder River with 100 people and tepees. Black Elk said, "It was just daybreak. There was a blizzard, and it was very cold. The people were sleeping. Suddenly, there were many shots and horses galloping through the village. It was the **cavalry** of the Wasichus, and they were yelling and shooting and riding their horses among the tepees. All the people rushed out and ran….The soldiers killed as many women and children and men as they could while the people were running toward a bluff. Then they set fire to some of the tepees and knocked the others down. But when the people were on the side of the bluff, Crazy Horse said something, and all the warriors began singing the death song and charged back upon the soldiers; and the soldiers ran."

After this battle, Black Elk's people then joined a large village on the Rosebud River made up of numerous Sioux tribes, including Hunkpapas, Minneconjous, Sans Arcs, Blackfeet, Brules, Santees, and Blue Clouds. Many great men were there, including Sitting Bull, Crazy Horse, and Spotted Eagle. The village was in the shape of a large oval, through which the river flowed. Another river, the Little Bighorn, was nearby.

One day in late June of 1876, Black Elk was with some boys watching the horses. He felt queer, like the times when he had had his visions. He knew something terrible was about to happen. It was hot. Many people were in the river; women were digging turnips. Suddenly, people shouted, "The chargers are coming!" A big cloud of dust was rising from the Hunkpapas' part of the village. Out of the dust came soldiers on big horses. A crowd of women and children ran downstream from the village. Black Elk and his brother made for a stand of timber,

This painting shows Custer's last stand, as Native American warriors overrun his soldiers' position. The defeat of the U.S. 7th Cavalry shocked the people of the United States. Although this was a great victory for the Sioux, it was in many ways a hollow victory also, as it led the U.S. government to work even harder to destroy the Native Americans' way of life.

where many of the Hunkpapas were. As the soldiers shot at them, the bullets made the leaves fall off the trees. Below him, it was like thunder with all the women and children of the village running; the warriors were on their ponies. A cry went up from those in the brush with Black Elk. "Take courage! Don't be a woman. The helpless are out of breath!"

Black Elk stayed in the woods a little while and thought of his vision. It made him feel strong. He saw his people as the powerful Thunder Beings and thought that the soldiers would be wiped out. Soon, another cry went up: "Crazy Horse is coming!" Toward the north and west, the people were yelling "Hoka hey!" and blowing on their eagle-bone whistles. To Black Elk, it sounded like a roaring wind. The village became dark with smoke and dust. There were many cries and the noise of horses' hooves and guns. Black Elk said, "I could hear the shod hooves of the soldiers' horses. The soldiers were running upstream, and we were all mixed there in the twilight and the great noise. Soon the soldiers were crowded into the river. Men and horses were all mixed up and fighting in the water."

Black Elk's friend, Standing Bear, was on top of a **butte**. He could see what was happening. A group of Custer's soldiers, commanded by Captain Marcus Reno, were attacking the village from the south. Custer led another group which attacked the village from the north. Standing Bear went down the butte to the mouth of a creek, then up a hill where the warriors were already fighting. He remembered, "They were ready for us and shooting. Our people were all around the hill on every side by this time. I heard some of our men shouting, 'They are gone!' And I saw that many of the soldiers' horses had broken loose and were running away. Everywhere our warriors began yelling, "Hoka hey! Hurry! Hurry!" Then we all went up, and it got dark with dust and smoke. I could see warriors flying around me like shadows, and the noise of all those hooves and guns and cries was so loud…the voices seemed to be on top of the cloud. It was like a bad dream."

Another warrior who lived through the battle, Iron Hawk, later said, "We saw soldiers…running downhill right towards us. Nearly all of them were afoot, and I think they were so scared that they didn't know what they were doing. [Eventually] the soldiers were all rubbed out and scattered around."

This great Sioux victory was the famous battle of the Little Bighorn. Custer and more than 200 soldiers were killed that day.

After the battle, the tribes stayed for a month near the Big Horn Mountains. In August, when they heard that the soldiers were coming again, the group headed east away from them. They burned the grass behind them so the soldiers' horses could not eat. Then it rained for days. Sitting Bull and his group left for Grandmother's Land (Canada). Those with Black Elk did not want to go. They had made a **treaty** with the white men only eight years before that said the land was theirs. But the white men ignored this. In September, the soldiers attacked the village, chasing the women and children from their tepees and taking all the dried bison meat they had stored for the winter to feed themselves. Crazy Horse came and chased the soldiers south toward the Black Hills.

THE NATIVE AMERICANS

When the warriors returned, the group started west again. The harsh winter came early. There were fewer than 2,000 people now. Many had gone over to join the whites. In November, news came that members of their tribe had sold the Black Hills. Black Elk said, "I learned when I was older that [most of] our people did not want to do this. The Wasichus went to some of the chiefs alone and got them to put their marks on the treaty. Maybe some of them did this when they were crazy from drinking [whiskey].... Only crazy or foolish men would sell their Mother Earth."

A chief named Spotted Tail came to try to make Black Elk's group surrender. He said many soldiers would come in the spring joined by Crows, Shoshones, and even Lakotas to fight them. The people with Black Elk were cold and hungry. They decided that surrendering was the best thing. They went to the fort. Later, the army decided to move them to the banks of the Missouri River.

In the early 1930s, Black Elk told a writer named John G. Neihardt about the Native American way of life and the changes he had witnessed during his lifetime. Neihardt reprinted his stories in the book *Black Elk Speaks: Being the Life Story of a Holy Man of the Oglala Sioux*, which was published in 1932. The book gives modern-day readers important insights into Native American culture, religion, and life on the Plains. It also shows how that way of life was destroyed during the late 19th century.

18

THE STORY OF BLACK ELK

However, the tribe did not want to go, so they broke away and traveled to Canada to join Sitting Bull. In Canada, Black Elk's powerful visions began to grow. The voices of the Thunder Beings told him things about the future. Eventually, Black Elk made his way back to his own country and began to heal people, becoming a medicine man.

When Black Elk was 16 years old, Buffalo Bill Cody was looking for Native Americans for his Wild West show. Black Elk decided to join him in order to see the world and learn things that could help his people. He traveled for three years, then he became so homesick, he had to return to America. When he came back, he learned that the Sioux leaders Crazy Horse and Sitting Bull had been killed.

By 1891, the fighting between whites and the Native Americans had mostly ended. The Native Americans who once had roamed the country freely were now forced to live on reservations, and were not allowed to follow their traditional ways. Black Elk lived his last years on the Pine Ridge Reservation in South Dakota. The culture and customs of the Native Americans had been destroyed by relative newcomers to the continent—the immigrants who came to settle in the United States and Canada during the 18th and 19th centuries.

A Native American people known today as the Hohokam once inhabited these prehistoric cliff dwellings in Colorado. The earliest Americans arrived on the continent more than 10,000 years ago.

2 Before European Dominance

When Europeans first arrived in North America, they encountered numerous well-established Native American cultures and societies. Where did these people come from and how did their societies develop?

During the last Ice Age, a "land bridge" existed between present-day Alaska and Siberia in Russia. People used this bridge to travel to North America to pursue game. Following their prey led them farther and farther into the interior. Eventually, they established settlements in Alaska, Canada, and along the northwestern coast of the United States. Some traveled all the way to Mexico and South America.

Over thousands of years, the climate became warmer. A wide variety of new plants began to grow. Animals like the ***woolly mammoth*** and ***mastodons*** grazed in herds. There were lions, camels, and saber-toothed tigers. Gradually, these animals disappeared. Although Native Americans still hunted small game, like antelope, deer, and waterfowl, they began to depend more on gathering the wild foods that grew on the land and fish and shellfish in the rivers, lakes, and seas. In most areas except the west, where they were ***nomadic***, tribes were living in established villages and farming a variety of crops.

The Copper Culture and the Mound Builders

Along Lake Superior in present-day Wisconsin, the Copper Culture began to make tools and other items out of copper over 6,500 years ago. These items included knife blades, axe heads, fishhooks, and jewelry. This group traded with other tribes as far away as the Atlantic coast and the Gulf of Mexico.

The Mound Builders built large mounds and lived in North America about 1,500 years ago. The mounds contained not only their dead, but also pottery, art objects, and jewelry. The two most prominent groups were the Hopewells and the Adena people. These groups lived in the Ohio River Valley and in the areas that now are the states of New York and Louisiana. The Great Serpent Mound the Adenas built is 20 feet wide, five feet high, and over one-quarter of a mile long. The Hopewells were a luxury-loving group who liked to wear fine furs, robes, earrings, and necklaces.

Ancient Indians of Mexico

Around 1200 B.C., northwest of the Yucatán Peninsula in Mexico, there existed an advanced civilization known as the Olmecs. For centuries, this culture's main population centers lay hidden by jungle growth and were only rediscovered during the modern era. The highly organized Olmecs developed an extensive trading network and built large temple pyramids. They also invented a numbering system, **hieroglyphs**, and a calendar. Perhaps the Olmecs' most striking achievement was the carving of huge stone heads, thought to be

BEFORE EUROPEAN DOMINANCE

The Great Serpent Mound in Adams County, Ohio, was built by the Adena people between 800 B.C. and A.D. 400. This historical earthwork is nearly a quarter of a mile long. It represents a giant snake holding an egg in its mouth.

This large sculpture from a Mayan site depicts Chac Mool, a messenger between humans and the gods. Offerings woud have been placed in the bowl at the center of the figure.

24

images of their leaders. How the Olmecs quarried 18-ton blocks and transported them 60 miles remains a mystery. The Olmec civilization disappeared around 700 B.C.

The Mayan civilization existed in Mexico about 1,000 years ago. Its main ceremonial center, Tikal, located at the base of the Yucatán Peninsula, had about 3,000 buildings in it, including six pyramids and seven temple palaces. Many stone carvings and other works of art were found here and at the other main population centers: Chichén Itza, Uxmal, and Copán. They reveal a high degree of workmanship and picture the magnificent lives of the rulers, with their plumed headdresses and **haughty demeanor**. The Mayan priests and engineers developed a highly advanced measurement of time, which included the concept of zero. Scientists remain mystified as to why the Mayan civilization suddenly disappeared around A.D. 900.

The center of the Teotihuacán civilization was the city of Teotihuacán. Teotihuacán was a true city in the modern sense. It had a population of 125,000 people and could accommodate an equal number during religious festivals. The city was centered around a two-mile-long boulevard called the Avenue of the Dead. Along this street were many temples, including the Temple of the Moon, which rose to a height of 150 feet. To the east and west were apartments and houses organized into sections by occupation. Pottery workers lived in a section separate from gem carvers; tanners lived in a different area. A system of waterways provided transportation in and around the city and irrigated the nearby fields. However, around 1,200 years ago the

These ancient cliff dwellings at Mesa Verde, Colorado, are thought to have been inhabited by the Anasazi in the 13th century.

Teotihuacán civilization disappeared.

The Aztec and Toltec civilizations, which developed in Mexico after these cultures, absorbed many of their influences. These advanced cultures also influenced the peoples of the Southwest and Mississippi River Valley areas of the United States.

Ancient Indians of the United States

Three cultures existed in the southwestern United States near the area where present-day New Mexico, Arizona, Colorado, and Utah come together. These cultures subsisted primarily on cultivating corn.

The peace-loving Hohokam people, their name meaning "The

Vanished Ones," grew crops by a large irrigation system. No evidence of warriors or warlike activity has been found in the archeological remains. The Mogollon people developed efficient "pit" houses that kept the occupants cool during the 100-degree days and warm during the chilly nights when temperatures often dropped below freezing. Members of both tribes were excellent craftsmen and artists.

Perhaps the most famous and controversial people in the area were the Anasazi (pronounced "Nasazi"). These people built large structures that resemble modern apartment complexes. One of these complexes was shaped in a semicircle that covered more than three acres. It had 660 rooms and was five stories tall. The Anasazi built other dwellings into the sides of cliffs and underneath rock ledges. About 700 years ago, at a structure known as Aztec Ruin, 2,000 inhabitants one day closed all windows and doors, put out their fires, and went away. They left all their possessions in place as if they intended to return, but they never did. Today's Hopi, Tewa, Kere, and Tano tribes are descendents of the ancient Anasazi.

In a number of places in the Mississippi River Valley, people who built "temple mounds" developed sophisticated cultures. The site known as Cahokia, near present-day East St. Louis, Illinois, is perhaps the most famous. In ancient times, the site was home to 40,000 people. Many smaller communities existed around Cahokia, and farmland spread out for hundreds of miles. The leaders and administrators lived in homes located on flat-topped, earthen mounds. By the 1500s, however, when Europeans began settling the area, Cahokia was already in ruins.

The arrival of Europeans during the 15th and 16th centuries, beginning with Christopher Columbus's landing on Caribbean islands in 1492, would change forever the lives of the native inhabitants of North and South America.

# 3 European Contact

At the time Christopher Columbus discovered the New World, a number of tribes flourished in an area bounded on the north by the Ohio River, on the east by the Atlantic Ocean, on the south by the Gulf of Mexico, and on the west by southeastern Texas. Creeks lived in present-day Alabama; Choctaw and Chickasaw in Mississippi; Seminoles in Florida; and Cherokee in Georgia and Tennessee. Abundant rainfall promoted thick forests and beautiful meadows. The balanced environment produced an abundance of edible wild grasses, nuts, and fruit. The forests teemed with game; the rivers and streams were filled with fish. The tribes developed a science of medicine, with many extracts having modern counterparts, such as aspirin and caffeine. Although they were often at odds, tribal warfare consisted mostly of small-scale raids. Casualties were few.

Eventually, the Spanish, French, and British began to take land from the Native Americans in the Southeast. The Spanish forced the people to work as slaves and disrupted village life by pitting one village against another. The Spanish also established missions where monks lived who changed the Native American way of life by converting the people to Christianity. The British and French used trade to gain control of the people, who went increasingly into debt as they traded furs and animal skins for knives, beads, and cloth.

29

Some of the tribes attempted to become more like the white settlers in order to maintain peace. Many Cherokees built houses and schools and became farmers. A man named Sequoya even created a written alphabet and published a newspaper. This did not satisfy the white settlers, however, who were now citizens of the newly formed United States. They continued to want more and more land. In 1830, President Andrew Jackson signed a law stating that all Native Americans were to be moved from their homes to lands far to the west. In a series of marches that became known as the Trail of Tears, the Choctaw, Creek, Cherokee, and Chickasaw people were forced to walk hundreds of miles. The journeys began in October and ended in February. Thousands died along the route because of the cold and shortages of food, clothing, and medical attention. When those that survived this ordeal arrived, they found no houses, no food, no farming tools, and no horses. A few tribes, like the Seminoles in Florida and some of the Choctaws, managed to remain in the Southeast by living in areas so remote that the white population could not find them.

The Northeastern and Great Lakes Tribes

A vast woodland once existed in what is now northeastern United States and southeastern Canada. The Atlantic Ocean was the eastern border, and the Great Lakes and Mississippi River marked the western border. The woods stretched along the northern shore of Lake Superior to Quebec province in Canada. The southern boundary was halfway through the states of Tennessee and North Carolina. The Delaware,

EUROPEAN CONTACT

As the United States grew during the early 19th century, its government decided it no longer wanted to share territory with the Native Americans. In the 1830s President Andrew Jackson signed the Indian Removal Act, which empowered the U.S. government to forcibly remove Native Americans from their lands. Thousands of Cherokee died on the long march from their homes in Georgia and Tennessee to the lands where the government wanted them to live in Oklahoma. The route became known as the Trail of Tears.

> Deer was the most sought-after game of the Southeastern tribes. Deer meat was a large part of their diet, and the skins were used to make clothing. Hunters stalked the animals by disguising themselves under deerskins. They also were masters at imitating deer calls. Before hunting, the hunter prayed to the spirit of the animals. This helped ensure that more deer would be born and that there would always be abundance.

Powhatan, and Montauk tribes dwelled on the fertile Atlantic coastal planes where they grew corn and other crops. The forest supplied ample game, while the clam beds along Long Island supplied shellfish. Lakes and rivers provided excellent transportation. Semi-nomadic groups, like the Abnaki and Penobscot, lived further north. Crops did not grow well in the rocky terrain there, so the natives hunted moose, beaver, deer, bear, and ducks. Because of their common language, all the tribes that lived in this region are known as the Algonquian.

Another group that lived in the area was the Iroquois. They had a different language and culture, and they lived in present-day upstate New York, in the St. Lawrence River Valley and around Lake Ontario and Lake Erie. The Iroquois were warlike and fiercely protected their land from outsiders, as well as between themselves. Fighting among the Iroquois tribes became so intense at one time that the members feared it would wipe out the people completely. According to legend, a Mohawk name Hiawatha traveled between the warring peoples and

EUROPEAN CONTACT

persuaded them to create the League of Iroquois. The League was comprised of five tribes: the Mohawk, the Senecas, the Oneidas, the Cayugas, and the Onondagas. By the mid-1600s, the Iroquois nation was the most powerful force in the woodlands. However, they, too, fell victim to the increasing tide of white settlers.

In the 1700s, the English colonies were expanding. Unlike the French, who wanted to trade for furs, the English colonists wanted land for crops, especially tobacco, which brought great profits in Europe. They saw the native cultures as an obstacle. The English colonies eventually rebelled to form the United States. The peace treaty signed in 1783 ending the American Revolutionary War also created a vast new American nation stretching west to the Mississippi River. Among the tribes that lived here were the Menominees, Illinois, Potawatomis, Ojibwas, Sauks, Ottawas, and Foxes.

In negotiations with the tribes, the United States government often used alcohol to persuade them. They "wined and dined" the chiefs,

---

During the American Revolution, most of the Iroquois sided with the British. Hundreds joined British soldiers and marched against American settlements in western New York and Pennsylvania. In retaliation, General George Washington sent an army against the Iroquois. With the destruction of 40 villages and most of their crops, it was the end of the Iroquois nation.

THE NATIVE AMERICANS

Black Hawk, a chief of the Sauk tribe, fought back against white settlers when his people were forced from their homes in Illinois. The Black Hawk War of 1832 did not last long; the Sauk and Fox Indians were quickly subdued and moved onto reservations.

who unknowingly gave up their homelands by signing treaties they did not understand. For example, in 1804, government officials invited representatives of the Fox and Sauk tribes to St. Louis. When they arrived, the officials served them alcohol and then persuaded them to sign a treaty giving the United States government control of all lands east of the Mississippi River. After this, the tribes moved west where they barely managed to survive. In 1832, a group of 1,000 men and women joined a Sauk chief named Black Hawk. Black Hawk did not want war, but simply wanted his people to be able to return to their homeland. He thought he could talk sense to the whites that were

EUROPEAN CONTACT

living in western Illinois. The whites found out, however, and mobilized a military group, called a militia. Because of the whites' attitude, Black Hawk soon realized that going back to his homeland was hopeless. He wanted to negotiate a peaceful return to the west bank of the Mississippi, but the whites began shooting at the Sauk and Fox.

Black Hawk led his warriors against the white settlers, killing 200, while losing 500 of his own people. In August 1832, the militia caught up with him as he was leading his people back through Iowa. Although Black Hawk attempted to surrender, the whites shot nearly all of the Native Americans as they tried to swim across the Mississippi. By 1835, the remaining Fox and Sauk rebels, along with members of the other tribes of the woodlands, had either been moved to lands west of the Mississippi or were forced to live on reservations within their former homelands.

Native American hunters pursue a herd of bison across the plains in this painting by Charles M. Russell. The bison, or buffalo, was very important to the Plains Indians' way of life.

4 The Natives of the West

The people of the Great Plains lived in an area that extended from northern Alberta and Saskatchewan in Canada to southern Texas. Its western border was the foothills of the Rocky Mountains. Its eastern border was the Mississippi River. Also known as the Great American Desert, the area receives only ten inches of rainfall a year. The Great Plains at one time was a vast grassland, ideal for the large herds of buffalo that thrived there.

The first Great Plains people were the Pawnees, Wichitas, and the Mandans. They hunted on foot, because they had no horses. Life on the Great Plains was **cyclical**. In late spring, after the tribe planted its crops, villages were moved temporarily onto the short-grass lands and hunting groups were formed. These returned when the hunt was over. In early autumn, when the crops were ready, the natives harvested them. Then the tribe went on a second hunt. Returning to the village, they made the buffalo hides and the skins of small game into shirts, **leggings**, tepee covers, and blankets. They dried the meat as a supply for the winter months.

Like other Native American groups, the people of the Great Plains saw their way of life end after they came into contact with American settlers. The white settlers' desire for more land was pitted against the native peoples' desire to retain their homelands. Both inflicted **atrocities**

THE NATIVE AMERICANS

Sitting Bull was a powerful and respected medicine man of the Hunkpapa Sioux. After the Sioux were forced onto reservations during the 1870s and early 1880s, Sitting Bull became an advocate for Native American rights. When white leaders feared the Plains Indians were preparing to revolt in 1890, they sent police to arrest him. Sitting Bull agreed to go peacefully, but he was shot and killed when some of his followers struggled with the arresting officers.

on one another. Altogether, the U.S. government spent millions of dollars and many years fighting the Native Americans. A more effective tactic, however, was the elimination of the buffalo herds. In 1800, there were 60 million buffalo living on the plains. By 1870, this number had dropped to 13 million. By 1900, there were fewer than 1,000 animals remaining when the government took steps to prevent them from becoming extinct. The slaughter began with the railroads, whose builders fed their laborers buffalo meat. Then whites began to kill the herds from the trains themselves, shooting them as "sport." The end came rapidly in the 1870s when a Pennsylvania company found it could tan the buffalo

THE NATIVES OF THE WEST

There are thousands of buffalo hides in this Kansas stockyard. As the buffalo were hunted nearly to extinction by whites, it became more difficult for the Native Americans of the Plains to maintain their traditional way of life.

hides into leather, and began offering $3 each for them. All these activities led directly to the end of the Great Plains people's way of life. Most were reduced to living on reservations, where a free and independent way of life was replaced by poverty and hopelessness.

The Southwest Native Americans

The Southwest tribes lived in present-day New Mexico, Arizona, and parts of southern California and Texas. Their lands contain the Grand Canyon, the Painted Desert, and the Río Grande and Colorado rivers. Little rain falls here, but when it does, floods occur. Temperatures are extremely hot during the day and are very cold at night. The Hopi, whose name means "Peaceful Ones," are one of a number of Pueblo tribes who have occupied this land longer than any North American people. Their apartment-like dwellings are similar to those of their Anasazi ancestors. They are built into cliffs or on top of **mesas**. The Hopi have always been farmers. They grow corn, squash, beans, and tobacco on the desert flatlands where runoffs and springs can water the crops.

In the 16th century, Spanish invaders attempted to change the Hopi's peaceful way of life. Intrigued by fantastic stories of seven pueblo cities constructed with jewels and streets paved with gold and silver, they first tried to subdue the Zuñi people, relatives of the Hopi. In 1540, Francisco Coronado mounted an expedition with 62 foot-soldiers, 230 horsemen in armor, and 1,000 Mexican Indians. The army carried muskets and swords, so the Zuñi did not win this encounter. When the invaders entered one of their villages, however, they were bitterly disappointed that it did not contain the gold, silver, and jewels they were seeking.

Forty years later, another Spanish force came to the area looking for land and slaves. They brought with them missionaries who wanted

---

Before the horse, moving the village to the hunting areas was not easy. Dogs were the only domesticated animals and beasts of burden. The villagers tied a *travois* to the dog, then loaded their belongings onto the travois. They sometimes had to walk many miles before encountering a herd of buffalo. After the Spanish introduced horses to the area, many of the plains tribes became expert horsemen and horse breeders.

to change the Native Americans into Christians. All kinds of torture and abuse, however, did not change the people, whose religion was the center of their lives. After years of unsuccessful attempts to throw off the Spanish intruders, a medicine man from the Rio Grande Pueblos named Popé led the people in an attack. After a week of fighting, the Spanish fled south to El Paso. In a number of other attacks in the years that followed, they were never able to subdue the Pueblo people.

The Navajo also live in this region. These people are fairly new to the desert lands, having first appeared there in the late 1400s. When they arrived, the Navajo were in awe of the Pueblo communities they saw and often attacked them. Eventually, the Navajos settled down; they lived in small family groups located miles away from each other. Their dwellings were called hogans, which were constructed out of wooden timbers, mud, and bark. The hogans were weatherproof and quite comfortable. The Navajo also kept herds of sheep whose wool they wove into blankets. Navajos are famous for the silver and *turquoise* jewelry they create. Other well-known tribes of the Southwest are the Apaches and Commanches.

The Great Basin

The Great Basin is bordered by the Sierra Nevada Mountains in the west and the Wasatch Mountains on the east. Its southern boundary is the edge of the Mojave Desert; the northern edge is the Snake River. It is home to a number of tribes who once were wandering desert dwellers. The Paiute, Ute, Gosiute, Shoshoni, and Bannock lived in this area for 10,000 years before whites arrived. This harsh land rarely receives more

THE NATIVE AMERICANS

A Spanish mission in California. The missions were built during the 18th century as centers from which Spanish priests could convert the Native Americans of the region to Christianity.

than seven inches of rainfall a year, but the people were able to survive. They ate **piñon** nuts, seeds, berries, fish, and rabbits. Because of the heat, they wore little clothing, except for rabbit skin cloaks that kept them warm during the cold nights. Their housing was a cone-shaped structure open at the top and made of willow poles and reeds.

The discovery of gold in California in 1848 marked the beginning of the end of these desert dwellers' way of life. Prospectors soon found silver and gold in Nevada, also. Settlers followed the prospectors. The whites cut down the piñon trees for fuel; their cattle trampled the berry and seed plots. Diseases, for which the Indians had no **immunity**, killed thousands. In their long history, these nomadic people had no reason to wage war, so they were not used to fighting. The United States government took over the land in 1863 without paying them any money and without a formal treaty, forcing the people to live on a reservation.

Indians of California

The Indians of present-day California lived in great abundance. Like today, frequent rain fed the streams and rivers and watered the land. A wide variety of animals and plants thrived. Pomos, Chumashes, Hupas, and Patwins lived in this area. Their homes were dome-shaped and had earthen ceilings and walls. In addition to salmon, the staple food was acorns, which were ground into flour.

The Spanish began to establish **missions** in the area starting in 1769. They built a string of these outposts along the coast and began to convert the Native Americans to Christianity. The Spanish changed the Indians' hunting-and-gathering way of life, forcing them to work at farming. As the years went by, the native languages, clothing, and many traditions were lost. Disease killed thousands. By the mid-1800s, most tribes were gone or near extinction. The exception were the Hupas, who lived in a hidden valley. When whites attempted to settle there, the United States sent troops to keep order. In 1864, the government made the area a reservation and paid the white settlers to leave. Today, the Hupas continue to live and prosper in their homeland.

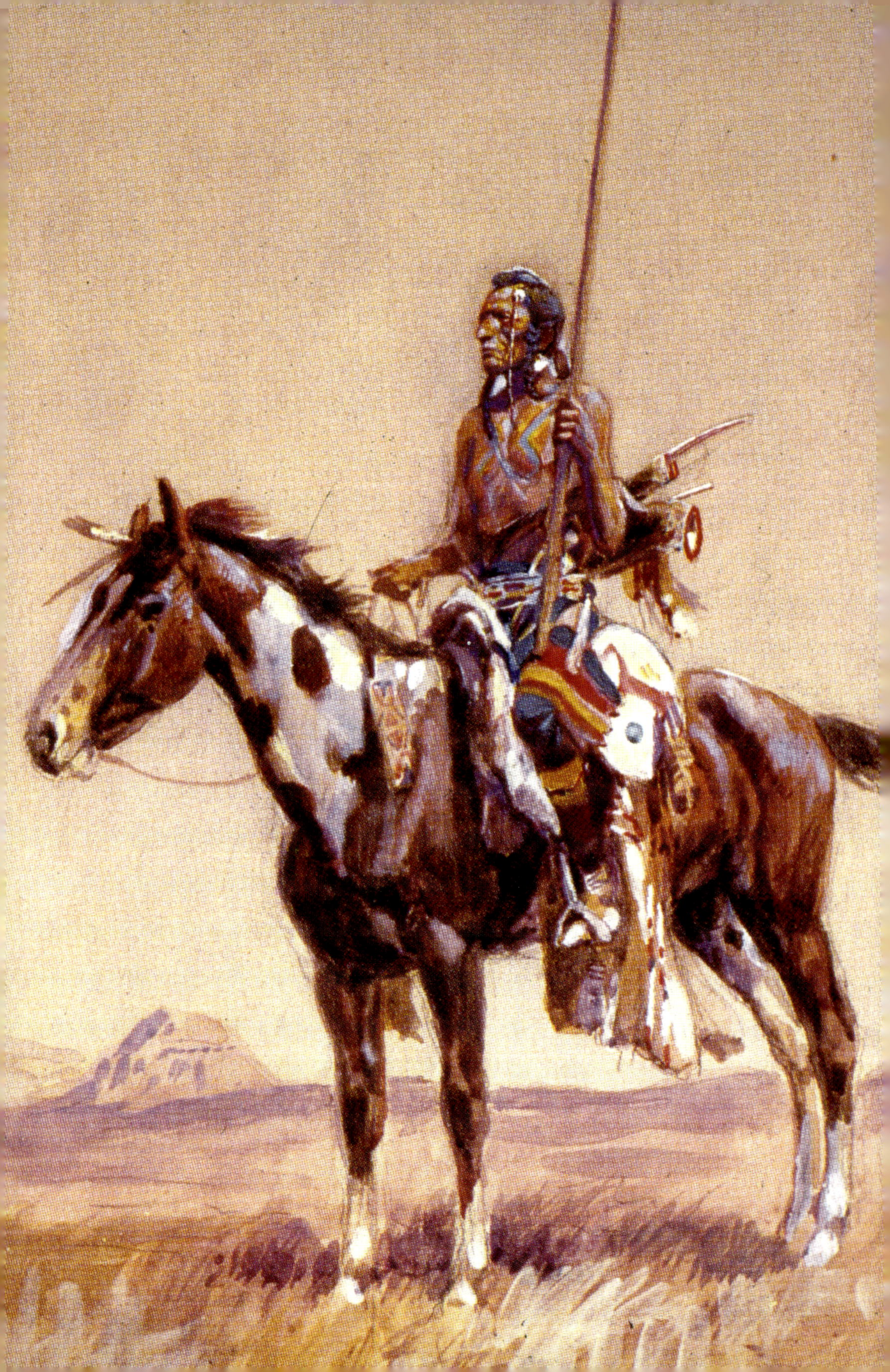

5 The Plateau Indians

In the high *plateau* country of the Fraser and Columbia river valleys were tribes who lived primarily by fishing the salmon that annually traveled up the streams. The weather was too cold for farming, so they gathered roots, berries, and nuts. The plateau area is bordered by the Cascade Mountains on the west and the Rocky Mountains on the east. The northern boundary is the Fraser River; the southern boundary is about halfway through the present-day states of Oregon and Idaho. It included sections of Montana, Washington, and British Columbia.

The tribes that lived here were the Walla Walla, Klamath, Cayuse, Nez Percé, Umatilla, and Klikitat, among others. Like other hunter-gatherer people, they lived a seasonal existence. They traveled to obtain food and returned to their homelands, which were located on riverbanks or in the river valleys. They smoked and dried salmon for later use, and ground the roots of the *camas* and other plants into flour. They lived in mat huts during the summer and partially underground earthen dwellings during the winter. The people were active

A Native American sits proudly on his horse. The Nez Percé were among the best horsemen of the northwest.

THE NATIVE AMERICANS

A Shoshone woman named Sacagawea served as a guide for the 1804–06 Lewis and Clark expedition. During this trip, a small group of men explored the vast western region that had recently been acquired from France in the Louisiana Purchase. The group followed the Columbia River until they reached the Pacific Ocean, then returned to St. Louis, their starting point. Sacagawea was a valuable member of the expedition. She was able to communicate with the Native Americans the explorers met, and in one case she saved a raft full of important notes and supplies from being swept away.

traders among themselves, and later, with white settlers. When the horse was introduced, the Cayuse, Yakima, Flathead, and Nez Percé adapted the animal to their use. The Nez Percé became perhaps the finest horsemen among the Native Americans.

In the late 1700s, tribes began to interact with whites. They contracted devastating diseases like smallpox and measles. After the famous U.S. government-sponsored Lewis and Clark expedition, farmers, railroaders, ranchers, and tradesmen began pouring into the region by way of the Oregon Trail. In a series of treaties, 370 altogether, the whites took over nearly all of their lands, leaving the reservations.

One of the last attempts by these Native Americans to hang on to their homelands was called the Nez Percé War. After signing away their beloved Wallowa River Valley in Oregon, the Nez Percé were supposed to move to poor lands in Idaho. Before they were scheduled to leave in 1877, white settlers stole a few Nez Percé horses. Young warriors killed some white settlers in retaliation, and the war was on. The tribe fought a running retreat, with soldiers pursuing them for 1,600 miles. Thirty miles before the tribe could reach **sanctuary** in Canada, the starving Nez Percé were trapped by U.S. troops. In his surrender speech, their leader, Chief Joseph said, "It is cold and we have no blankets. The little children are freezing to death. My people…have run away to the hills and have no blankets, no food. I want to have time to look for my children and see how many of them I can find. Maybe I shall find them among the dead. Hear me, my chiefs. I am tired; my heart is sick and sad. From where the sun now stands, I will fight no more forever."

THE NATIVE AMERICANS

A colored postcard pictures Chief Joseph, leader of the Nez Percé. The tribe attempted to escape U.S. soldiers by crossing into Canada. However, after a 1,600-mile journey they were stopped just 30 miles from the border, and forced to return to a reservation in the United States.

The Natives of the Northwest Coast

The Chinook, Kwakiutl, and Tlingit lived on the ocean coasts of northwestern Canada and the United States. The forests were so thick and the land was so rugged that hunting for deer, elk, bear, and smaller animals was only possible during the winter when the snow drove the game down to the flat areas. The people had almost no agriculture. Instead, they lived on the cod, herring, trout, halibut, and shellfish that abounded in this water-rich area. Their main food source was the salmon that traveled up the streams and rivers every spring to ***spawn***. This fish provided not only most of the food, but also oil.

In the late 17th century, Russian traders began to visit the area. They noticed that sea otters lived there in abundance. Soon, word spread. The Spanish, English, French (and later the Americans) all wanted to trade with the northwest tribes in order to get these valuable furs. The coastal natives were shrewd bargainers who greatly increased their wealth by obtaining knives, glass beads, and blankets from the Europeans for furs. In a ceremony called a "potlatch," the coastal Native Americans would show off their wealth to their visitors. These elaborate events often lasted 12 days or longer, and were times of great ceremony, the telling of legends, exchanging gifts, and feasting. Potlatches were usually held to acknowledge a marriage, the death of an important person, or a new chief. Christian people thought that these were old, wasteful practices. In 1884, the Canadian government, which controlled most of the land where the coastal tribes lived, outlawed potlatches. The natives continued to practice them, however. After many years, the Canadian government gave up its attempt to outlaw these events.

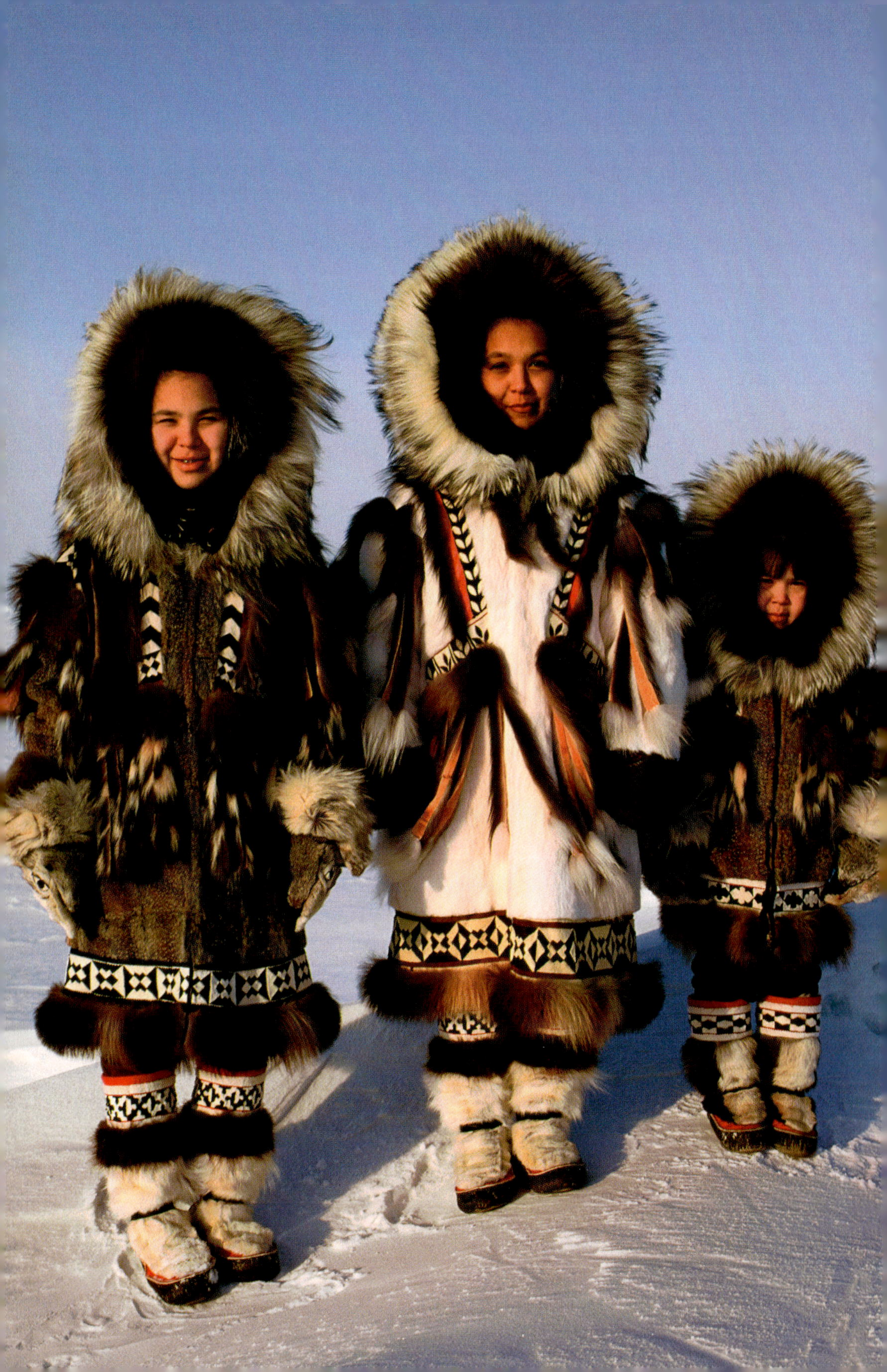

6 The Subarctic People

Tribes that live in the subarctic are the Cree, Chipewyan, Ojibwa, Kutchin, Slave, Dogrib, and others. The harsh land they occupy covers the interiors of Alaska and Canada. To the north lies mile upon mile of treeless flat land mixed with small hills, through which flow numerous streams and rivers. The vast area is dotted with small lakes and ponds. Plants bloom briefly in the short summers, attracting the *caribou*. Clouds of black flies and mosquitoes often fill the air. Winter is extremely cold and windy; the rivers and lakes freeze to a depth of five feet. The southern area is mostly pine and spruce forest that stretches from the Atlantic Ocean to the Rockies.

Since ancient times, the caribou provided most of the people's needs. No part of the animal went to waste. The hide was made into leggings, skirts, tent coverings, and blankets. The bones were used for clubs and tools. The meat and organs were a main source of food. The tribes followed the migrating animals, supplementing their diet by fishing and hunting small mammals. They made snowshoes and household items out of spruce and willow, and canoes out of birchbark.

These Inuit children in Alaska are dressed warmly against the cold subarctic weather.

THE NATIVE AMERICANS

This group of Inuits was photographed in 1914, when they visited the camp of Vilhjalmur Stefanson, a Canadian explorer and writer. Stefanson became known for his books about the Inuit culture.

Contact with Europeans changed the subarctic people's way of life. Previously, they had been self-sufficient. They made their own clothing and tools, gathered their own food, and traded with each other. When they began trading beaver furs for manufactured items like guns, wool blankets, glass beads, knives, and cooking utensils, it was no longer necessary to follow the herds of caribou. Instead, they began to settle in permanent villages. Wooden houses replaced their skin-covered tent dwellings. After the beaver almost became extinct from over-hunting, the people could no longer trade. The harsh climate prevented them from farming. Like other Native Americans, alcohol and disease took its toll. The government has stepped in to provide medical attention, schools, and welfare money, but many traditions have become lost.

People of the Arctic

The Arctic region stretches 5,000 miles across the top part of Canada to the western coasts of Alaska. It is an area of rapid rivers and jagged mountain ranges. In the south, there are some trees, but to the north, where most of the people of this region live, the area is treeless. The main habitable lands are the rolling, rocky, barren plains called the ***tundra***. For most of the year, the soil of the tundra is covered with snow and ice. In the short summer, the snow and ice melts. The deeper soil, called permafrost, does not melt, however, and water tends to remain on top. The water then mixes with soil. This converts the tundra into a wet, muddy marsh, which breeds swarms of mosquitoes and makes travel difficult.

The word "Eskimo" means "raw flesh eaters," a name the Algonquian Indians gave to them. The world knows them by this name, but they call themselves the Inuit ("The People"). The Inuit have lived in this cold and hostile climate for 30 centuries. They traditionally used dog sleds for transportation and built igloos out of snow and ice to protect them from the winter winds and storms. To the north of the tundra lies the Arctic Ocean. It is the home of seal, walrus, and whales, which were essential for the Eskimos' survival. The animals not only provided the people with food, but also with oil for light and heat, skins for clothing and tents, and bones for tools, decorations, cooking implements, and weapons.

As a migrating people, Eskimos hunted seal, walrus, and whale in the winter. In the spring, they fished for cod and other fish, and hunted for small game like white fox and squirrel. In summer, they fished salmon from the streams and hunted the caribou that were migrating north. Contact with European white settlers and traders, however, dramatically changed their way of life. In the early 19th century, they

An Inuit hunter lowers himself behind a white board, which provides camouflage as he waits for game to appear in this photograph from the 1920s. Contact with Europeans changed the way of life followed by both the subarctic and arctic Native American tribes.

began to trade fur, whale oil, and skins for guns, kettles, and knives. Eskimos could earn $200 a week during the whaling season working as travel guides and deckhands on ships. This allowed them to live comfortably the rest of the year. The rifles that they obtained through trading altered traditional hunting patterns. They could take as many caribou as they needed with these guns, no longer having to make their own spears and harpoons.

White society also brought liquor and diseases. Missionaries converted many to the Christian faith, so the Eskimos abandoned most of their **taboos**, **amulets**, and beliefs. Today, the Inuit live in wood houses heated with oil or wood. They use snowmobiles instead of dog sleds. Motorboats have replaced **kayaks**. Their clothing is made of cotton or wool rather than from caribou and sealskins. Seeing these changes, one scientist stated, "They may speak the Eskimo language still. They may still roam the hunting grounds of their forefathers. But most of them are Eskimos no longer."

Famous Native Americans

Geronimo, Apache warrior

Sitting Bull, Sioux medicine man and chief

Crazy Horse, Sioux chief who defeated General Custer at the battle of the Little Bighorn

Cochise, Apache chief

Sacagawea, Shoshone woman who guided the Lewis and Clark expedition

Pocahontas, daughter of the famous Algonquian chief Powhatan, she married an English settler named John Rolfe

Jim Thorpe, gold-medal-winning Olympic champion in the pentathlon and decathlon

Sequoyah, developed the written Cherokee language; also published a Cherokee newspaper

Popé, Pueblo leader who defeated the Spanish

Montezuma, Aztec ruler

Chief Joseph, Nez Percé who led his people in defending their homeland

Russell Means, modern-day Native American activist

The Apache chief Geronimo led a series of wars against white settlers in Arizona and New Mexico during the 1870s and 1880s. He eventually surrendered, and died in 1909 on a reservation in Oklahoma.

Chronology

50,000 B.C. People cross land bridge to North America in search of game.

10,000 B.C. Woolly mammoths, camels, lions, and tigers live in North America.

4,500 B.C. Copper Culture exists in Wisconsin.

1,200 B.C. Olmec civilization begins in Mexico.

A.D. 500 Mound Builders live in Ohio River Valley.

1000 Mayan civilization begins in Mexico; the Hopi establish villages in the "four corners" area of the United States.

1492 Christopher Columbus discovers the New World.

1540 Spanish military under Francisco Coronado attacks Pueblo villages.

1650 The League of the Iroquois is the most powerful woodland nation.

1769 The Spanish build the first California missions.

1783 The American Revolutionary War ends; the United States is created.

1800 Sixty million buffalo roam the Great Plains.

1830 President Andrew Jackson orders all Native Americans removed to lands west of the Mississippi River.

1870 The number of buffalo is 13 million.

1900 The number of buffalo is 1,000.

1920 Total U.S. Native American population is less than 250,000.

1953 The government begins "terminating" tribes. Native Americans are expected to move to cities and get jobs. The project is a disaster for Indians.

1957 Congress stops termination unless a tribe requests it.

1961 Native American leaders publish a "Declaration of Indian Purpose," that calls for the government to give back lost reservations and restore Indian rights. Indians begin demonstrating to demand changes.

2008 Total Native American population in the United States and Canada is estimated at more than 2.9 million.

57

Glossary

Amulet an object worn on the body supposedly having magical power that guards against injury or evil.

Atrocity an act characterized by cruel, brutal behavior.

Butte a steep hill standing alone on a plain, especially in a desert area.

Camas a plant of the lily family that has sweet, edible bulbs.

Caribou a large deer that lives in the north, closely related to the reindeer.

Cavalry an army troop mounted on horseback.

Cyclical occurring in a regular, set period of time.

Demeanor outward behavior or conduct.

Haughty showing great pride.

Hieroglyphs pictures or symbols that represent words, used instead of alphabetic letters.

Immunity the ability to fight disease.

Kayak a narrow enclosed canoe, originally made of sealskin and wood, that transports one or two people.

Leggings a leather garment that protects the legs.

Mastodon a large mammal that resembled an elephant, except it had a larger head and different teeth. It is now extinct.

Mesa a small, high, flat area of land that has steep sides.

Mission the dwelling place of a group of people whose purpose is to teach others their religion.

Nomadic wandering, not belonging to a permanent settlement.

Piñon a type of pine tree that grows in the southwest United States.

Plateau an elevated piece of level land.

Sanctuary a place of safety and protection.

Spawn to produce or deposit eggs.

Taboo sacred rules that people of a tribe or other group cannot break.

Travois a contraption for transporting items, consisting of a net or platform between two poles. One end is tied to a dog or horse near the shoulders; the other end is dragged along the ground.

Treaty a negotiated agreement set in writing, usually between two or more political authorities.

Tundra vast treeless plain of the Arctic region.

Turquoise a greenish-blue semiprecious stone.

Vision when someone sees something other than by normal sight, as in a dream about the future.

Woolly mammoth an ancient elephant, now extinct, that had tusks that curved upward and hairy skin.

Further Reading

Catlin, George. *North American Indians*. New York: Penguin Books, 1989.

Champagne, Duane. *Native America—Portrait of the Peoples*. Detroit: Invisible Ink Press, 1994.

Gibson, Arrell Morgan. *The American Indian*. Lexington: D.C. Heath and Company, 1980.

Oswalt, Wendell H. *This Land Was Theirs*. Mountain View: Mayfield Publishing Company, 1988.

Spicer, Edward H. *The American Indians*. Cambridge: Harvard University Press, 1980.

Turner, Geoffrey. *Indians of North America*. Dorset: Blandford Press, 1979.

Weatherford, Jack. *First Nations—Firsthand*. Cameron Fleet, Ed. Edison: Chartwell Books, Inc., 1997.

Finding Your Native American Ancestors

Byers, Paula K. *Native American Genealogical Sourcebook*. Detroit: Gale Research, 1995.

Carmack, Sharon DeBartolo. *A Geneaologist's Guide to Discovering Your Immigrant and Ethnic Ancestors*. Cincinnati: Betterway Books, 2000.

McClure, Tony Mack. *Cherokee Proud: A Guide for Tracing and Honoring Your Cherokee Ancestors*. Somerville, Tenn.: Chunannee Books, 1997.

Internet Resources

http://www.census.gov

The official Web site of the U.S. Bureau of the Census contains information about the most recent census taken in 2000.

http://www12.statcan.ca/english/census/index.cfm

The Web site for Canada's Bureau of Statistics, which includes population information updated for the most recent census in May 2006.

http://virginiaindians.pwnet.org/

A Web site dedicated to the many Native Americans tribes of Virginia.

http://www.doi.gov/bureau-indian-affairs.html

The official Web site of the United States Department of the Interior Bureau of Indian Affairs.

http://www.curtis-collection.com/curtis/

This Web site features the work of Edward S. Curtis, who visited and photographed 80 western Native American tribes from 1890 – 1930.

http://www.americanindians.com/

This Web site provides information about all the different tribes within the Northern Hemisphere.

Publisher's Note: The Web sites listed on this page were active at the time of publication. The publisher is not responsible for Web sites that have changed their address or discontinued operation since the date of publication. The publisher reviews and updates the Web sites each time the book is reprinted.

Index

Abnaki tribe, 32
Adena tribe, 22
Algonquian tribe, 32, 53
American Revolutionary War, 33
Anasazi tribe, 27
Apache tribe, 41
Atlantic Ocean, 22, 29, 30, 51
Aztec tribe, 26

Bannock tribe, 41
Black Elk, 11–19
Black Hawk, 34–35
Black Hills, 13–14, 18
Blackfeet tribe, 14
Blue Cloud tribe, 14
British, 29, 33, 49
Brule tribe, 14

Cahokia, 27
Canada, 18–19, 21, 30, 37, 47, 48–49, 51, 53
Cayuga tribe, 33
Cayuse tribe, 45–47
Cherokee tribe, 29, 30
Chickasaw tribe, 29, 30
Chief Joseph, 47
Chinook tribe, 48
Chipewyan tribe, 51
Choctaw tribe, 29, 30
Christianity, 29, 40, 43, 49, 55
Chumash tribe, 43
Cody, William (Buffalo Bill), 19
Columbus, Christopher, 29
Commanche tribe, 41
Copper Culture, 22
Coronado, Francisco, 40
Crazy Horse, 14, 16, 18, 19
Cree tribe, 51
Creek tribe, 29, 30
Crow tribe, 18
Custer, George Armstrong, 12, 17

Delaware tribe, 30
Dogrib tribe, 51

Europeans, 21, 49, 52, 54

Flathead tribe, 47
Fox tribe, 33, 34–35
French, 29, 33, 49

Gosiute tribe, 41
Great Serpent Mound, 22
Gulf of Mexico, 22, 29

Hiawatha, 32
Hohokam tribe, 26
Hopewell tribe, 22
Hopi tribe, 27, 40–41
Hunkpapa Sioux tribe, 14, 16
Hupa tribe, 43

Illinois tribe, 33
Inuit tribe (Eskimo), 53
Iron Hawk, 17

Jackson, Andrew, 30

Kere tribe, 27
Klamath tribe, 45
Klikitat tribe, 45
Kutchin tribe, 51
Kwakiutl, 48

Lakota (Oglala Sioux) tribe, 13, 14, 19
League of Iroquois, 32–33
Lewis and Clark expedition, 47
Little Bighorn, 16–17
Little Powder River, 11, 14

Mandan tribe, 37
Mayan tribe, 25
Menominee tribe, 33
Mexico, 21–26
Minneconjou Sioux tribe, 14
Mogollon tribe, 27
Mohawk tribe, 32, 33
Montana, 11–13
Montauk tribe, 32
Mound Builders, 22

Native Americans, 21, 29–30, 37, 40, 43, 47, 49, 53
Navajo tribe, 41
Nez Percé tribe, 45–47
Nez Perce War, 47
North America, 21, 40

Olmec tribe, 22–25
Ojibway tribe, 33, 51
Oneida tribe, 33
Onondaga tribe, 33
Ottowa tribe, 33

62

Paiute tribe, 41
Patwin tribe, 43
Pawnee tribe, 37
Penobscot tribe, 32
Pomos tribe, 43
Popé, 41
Potawatomis tribe, 33
Powhatan tribe, 32
Pueblo tribe, 40–41

Red Cloud, 13–14
Reno, Marcus, 16
Rosebud River, 14
Russians, 48

San Arc Sioux tribe, 14
Santee tribe, 14
Sauk tribe, 33, 34–35
Seminole tribe, 29, 30
Seneca tribe, 33
Sequoya, 30
Shoshone tribe, 18, 41
Sitting Bull, 14, 19
Slave tribe, 51
South America, 21

Spanish, 29, 40–41, 43, 49
Spotted Eagle, 14
Spotted Tail, 18
Standing Bear, 16

Tano tribe, 27
Teotihuacán, 25
Tewa tribe, 27
Tlingit tribe, 48
Toltec tribe, 26
Trail of Tears, 30

Umatilla tribe, 45
United States, 21, 26, 30, 33, 34, 37, 43, 47, 48
Ute tribe, 41

Walla Walla tribe, 45
Wichita tribe, 37

Yakima tribe, 47
Yucatán Peninsula, 22, 25

Zuñi tribe, 40

Photo Credits

Page
2: Hulton/Archive/Getty Images
10: North Wind Picture Archives
13: Denver Public Library
15: Little Bighorn Battlefield National Monument/National Park Service
20: Papilio/Corbis
23: Hulton/Archive/Getty Images
24: Corbis Images
26: Hulton/Archive/Getty Images
28: Hulton/Archive/Getty Images
31: The Woolaroc Museum, Bartlesville, Oklahoma
34: Hulton/Archive/Getty Images
36: Hulton/Archive/Getty Images
38: Denver Public Library
39: National Archives
42: Richard Cummins/Corbis
44: Amon Carter Museum
46: Hulton/Archive/Getty Images
48: Hulton/Archive/Getty Images
50: Galen Rowell/Corbis
52: Hulton/Archive/Getty Images
54: Hulton/Archive/Getty Images
56: Arizona Historical Society

Contributors

Barry Moreno has been librarian and historian at the Ellis Island Immigration Museum and the Statue of Liberty National Monument since 1988. He is the author of *The Statue of Liberty Encyclopedia*, which was published by Simon & Schuster in October 2000. He is a native of Los Angeles, California. After graduation from California State University at Los Angeles, where he earned a degree in history, he joined the National Park Service as a seasonal park ranger at the Statue of Liberty; he eventually became the monument's librarian. In his spare time, Barry enjoys reading, writing, and studying foreign languages and grammar. His biography has been included in *Who's Who Among Hispanic Americans*, *The Directory of National Park Service Historians*, *Who's Who in America*, and *The Directory of American Scholars*.

Richard A. Bowen is a Wisconsin author whose books include *The Art of Hearing: Seven Practical Methods for Improving Your Hearing*, *Meeting Your Match—His Story*, and *Spirit and Nature*, a book of verse. He is co-owner of Ariadne Publishers and editor of the "Spiritual Awakenings" quarterly.

AUG 2 6 2009
2295